T0051513

the FRENCH 75

the
FRENCH
75

JOHN MAXWELL HAMILTON

LOUISIANA STATE UNIVERSITY PRESS
BATON ROUGE

Published with the assistance of The Noland Fund

Published by Louisiana State University Press
lsupress.org

Copyright © 2024 by John Maxwell Hamilton
All rights reserved. Except in the case of brief quotations used in articles or
reviews, no part of this publication may be reproduced or transmitted in any format
or by any means without written permission of Louisiana State University Press.

Manufactured in the United States of America
First printing

Designer: Barbara Neely Bourgoyne
Typeface: Arno Pro
Printer and binder: Integrated Books International (IBI)

Cover illustration courtesy Sam Gregory Anselmo.

Library of Congress Cataloging-in-Publication Data
Names: Hamilton, John Maxwell, author.
Title: The French 75 / John Maxwell Hamilton.
Other titles: French seventy-five
Description: Baton Rouge : Louisiana State University Press, 2024.
Identifiers: LCCN 2023045546 | ISBN 978-0-8071-8176-8 (cloth)
Subjects: LCSH: Cocktails. | Cocktails—History.
Classification: LCC TX951 .H2239 2024 | DDC 641.87/409—dc23/eng/20240108
LC record available at https://lccn.loc.gov/2023045546

for Bettsie

CONTENTS

the FRENCH 75

INTRODUCTION
L'AFFAIRE DES SOIXANTE-QUINZE

In early 1749 a poem chiding Louis XV came to the attention of the court in Versailles. It called the king a "monster" for dismissing a longtime minister. The police were mobilized to find "the source of such an infamy." The royal spy network was put on the case. The king followed the investigation closely. By the end, the authorities had thrown not one, but fourteen subversives into the Bastille. None of these culprits, however, was the originator of the poem.

L'Affaire des Quatorze was a tangle. The rebellious verses changed as they passed from person to person.

Sometimes the malefactors scribbled the mocking lines on bits of paper. Mostly, though, people with a good memory and a facility for improvisation recited or sang them to entertain friends.

Further confounding their inquiry, the police discovered five other distinct traitorous poems reverberating through the streets of Paris. Further still, the poetry not only sounded in the halls of Versailles but also had origins there, where factions used it to settle scores and vie for power.

This, as Robert Darnton notes in his history of L'Affaire des Quatorze, was "a case of collective creation."

The French 75 cocktail is also such a story. The cocktail is subversive in its potency. Novelist Alec Waugh called it "the most powerful cocktail in the world." It is self-perpetuating, elusively morphing into new forms. One is reminded of a comment by the marquis who oversaw the investigation of L'Affaire des Quatorze. The satirical poems were "raining down from everywhere." Depending on how they are prepared, the 75 cocktails that inundate bars can be refreshing or luscious—or insipid.

The French 75 cocktail began in France during the Great War. It was named after a new, powerful, and celebrated weapon, the French 75 artillery piece. From the very first, bartenders tinkered with the recipe. Their successors never stopped. Today we are witnessing an explosion of creativity, perhaps most notably emanating from Arnaud's Restaurant in New Orleans. Riffing on the cocktail like an improvisational second-line jazz band that follows the permit-holding main line in New Orleans parades, it established the French 75 as a signature Big Easy libation and stimulated its spread nationally.

The French 75's peripatetic journey is bewildering. It's impossible to establish exactly when or in what precise place it was first served; there is no consensus on what form of the cocktail should be called *the* French 75. "The most controversial cocktail ever," says Katy Casberian, an owner of Arnaud's. "It's crazy."

Like L'Affaire des Quatorze, this is an in-search-of book. The exploration begins in Europe. We'll bounce between Paris and London, as well as detour to such other climes as Singapore to consider French 75 variations. Stateside, we'll check into the New York history of the cocktail, invent a new recipe in Washington, DC, make a revealing stop in Aurora, Illinois, and end up in New Orleans, after which we will be ready to assess the best recipes. By the end of the trip, we also will have discovered a good deal about cocktail culture generally.

I was an ingénue in cocktail journalism when I embarked on this search. But an interest in alcoholic beverages and sleuthing is embedded in my pedigree. Whether chicha in the Andes or chacha in Republic of Georgia villages, I've used my reporting trips abroad to explore local spirits. My great-grandfather, Irishman Tom Curran, showed the way. He was a member of the Moorhead, Minnesota, police force and part owner of the Three Orphans Saloon—and perhaps brothel. (Memories are conveniently vague on this last bit, as the bar all by itself was a sore point for my very Catholic great-grandmother and other ladies in the family.) Curran was skilled in rectification, the process of blending various whiskies into a smooth house blend.

I also happened to have a non-cocktail-related qualification for writing this book—although I did not realize this until the search was underway. I had written extensively about propaganda. Cocktails, I soon discovered, are lavishly garnished with publicity, as well as its close relatives ballyhoo, hype, spin, pseudo-event, puffery, hoopla, and hooey. The first French 75 was, in fact, a product of World War I propaganda.

With this in mind, we start rectifying L'Affaire des Soixante-Quinze with a look at the razzmatazz cocktail culture that the French 75 epitomizes.

CHAPTER ONE

THE BOOZE ARTS

"In the department of conviviality," H. L. Mencken wrote in his tour de force *The American Language,* "the imaginativeness of Americans was early shown both in the invention and in the naming of new and often highly complex beverages." Americans coined *saloon-keeper* and *bartender.* Mencken rejoiced that homegrown behind-the-mahogany wizards were superior to the British in this regard. "Seeking a name, for example, for a mixture of whiskey and soda-water," he wrote, "the best [the British] could achieve was *whiskey-and-soda*." The Americans called it a *highball.*

Mencken liked the names *phlegm-cutter, corpse-reviver, blind pig,* and *Mamie Taylor,* among many, many other cocktails that floated into saloons in the early nineteenth century. He thought the cocktail was "the greatest of all the contributions of the American way of life to the salvation of mankind."

The Sage of Baltimore spoke of saloons from deep personal experience. He had strong views on the "Booze Arts." He put the "silly" word *mixologist* in the same category as *mortician* for undertaker, *whooptician* for a college cheerleader, and "*colonel* for a whiskey drummer." Though a careful etymologist, he used the barroom as a launching pad for flamboyant flights of imagination. He claimed to have commissioned a mathematician to calculate how many different cocktails could be made from the ingredients in a good bar. The answer was 17,864,392,788. "I have myself invented eleven," Mencken wrote, "and had nine named after me."

* * *

COCKTAIL ANARCHY

One can get only so far looking for the headwaters of saloon words before the trails become poorly marked and the wrangling breaks out. "Pitfalls, booby traps, and other difficulties," Mencken wrote in the *New Yorker*, "strew the path of anyone seriously interested in the origin and history of booze terms."

The Mamie Taylor cocktail is one such poorly mapped beverage. Taylor, known for the ditty "Hoity Toity," was a turn-of-the-twentieth-century comic actress of that name—or nearly that name. Her real name was Mayme, not Mamie. The Herodotus of this sloppy story was her publicist. While on a boat trip on Lake Ontario, the publicist said, she tweaked a drink served to her by accident. The bartender named it after her. The alleged alteration (by adding a lemon peel to Scotch and ginger ale, although lime juice was often used instead) was modest. Mayme Taylor and the drink reinforced each other's celebrity, which was abetted by journalists with a sense of humor. The cocktail was so famous in Washington, a local reporter wrote, "extra bartenders have been placed on duty in all the larger buffets."

As this book was being written, the *New York Times* witnessed a modern cocktail unveiling that involved a performer and a publicist. (You may see a pattern here.) Singer-actress Kylie Minogue staged the show at Bemelmans Bar in New York's Carlyle Hotel. "A publicist had described Ms. Minogue as a practiced bartender with a specialty drink," the *Times* reported. But the actual author of the Pink Pearl was Abdul Rashid, the hotel bartender. Ms. Minogue did not know how to mix the drink and fumbled when she strained it into a glass. Her only authentic connection to the Pink Pearl was that she made herself look like the beverage by wearing a jacket of that hue. The *Times* story set the record straight—for now. Who knows for how long?

Cocktail culture is not, shall we say, rigid. French standards for wine are detailed, which is not surprising since the French have rules for how much boiled egg a kindergarten student may be fed for lunch. United States government-enforced rules for whiskey distilling are specific on the length of aging required and what barrels must be used. "Government made bourbon better," says my friend Kevin Kosar, an expert on our political system as well as author of *Whiskey: A Global History*. But such regulations only deal with what goes into the bottle and how it is labeled. They don't place limits on how it must be poured or what it may be called when it's in a glass.

Bartenders have occasionally fought the resulting anarchy, but with limited results. In the 1930s the United Kingdom Bartenders Guild published *Approved Cocktails*. The book's recipes did not include the French 75. To get that, one had to write a letter to the guild. It was much easier to make up your own version and a story to go with it.

"Bartending is not an academic discipline, and many people stick with their favorite old stories and favorite old sources without worrying too much about keeping up with the literature," David Wondrich told me. Wondrich, a former English professor, is one of the most highly respected producers of cocktail literature. Careful about being misunderstood, he added, "many terrifyingly smart" bartenders are as attentive to detail as a microbiologist. In other words, they measure carefully. How they talk about cocktails is a different matter altogether.

Jerry Thomas, a nineteenth-century phenom, is acclaimed as America's first great cocktail microbiologist. Author of the first-known American cocktail guide, Wondrich says, he "did more than anyone else to establish a canon of American drinks." He was a showman. He had bowling lanes in one of his saloons, etchings, and a statue of himself. He was famous for the Blue Blazer, a flaming concoction that he tossed back and forth between silver shakers. He did not deserve credit for inventing that cocktail, although it is often said he did, and he falsely claimed to have created the Tom and Jerry cocktail. Gin advertisers touted yet another canard, that Thomas invented the Martini.

THE APPEARANCE OF
THE FRENCH 75

To turn to the French 75, what do we know for sure? The earliest-known reference to it is in O. O. McIntyre's syndicated column, "New-York-Day-by-Day," which appeared in the *Washington Herald* on December 2, 1915:

> There has been brought back to Broadway from the front by War Correspondent E. Alexander Powell the Soixante-Quinze cocktail—the French seventy-five. It is one-third gin, one-third grenadine, one-third applejack and a dash of lemon juice. Frank Leon Smith, the story writer, says he drank one and immediately paid his rent.

Powell was in New York to speak in connection with a French propaganda motion picture, "Fighting in France." Powell's paper, the *New York World,* sponsored the showings. Short story writer Frank Leon Smith had just turned his talents to writing silent movie subtitles in order to pay the rent. He later wrote successful film scripts for talkies and improved his housing further by purchasing a farm in the Catskill Mountains.

The next year, 1916, a British magazine *Sphere* noted the mood in war-weary Paris: "The only indication of levity which any restaurant manifests is a cocktail invented by the mixer of the American bar at Ciro's, called a 'soixante-quinze,' an agreeable blend of Calvados apple brandy and other mysterious ingredients." Ciro's was a booming restaurant-bar that opened in 1912.

No one doubts the cocktail got its name from the French 75-millimeter artillery piece, which Powell saw blazing away when the cocktail also burst forth. But the *Sphere*'s attribution of the drink's invention to Ciro's bartender is otherwise unsubstantiated and dubious. In this and many other ways, L'Affaire des Soixante-Quinze presents a special problem to saloon sleuths. For one thing, the French 75 does not follow the usual pattern when it comes to naming derivative cocktails. Typically the modification of an established drink leads to a new name. This makes sense. You don't get much fame for inventing the Martini XII. You need to jigger the name as well. When American diplomat Hugh Gibson introduced a pickled onion to a Martini—this is my preferred guess as to the pioneer of this cocktail—the drink became a Gibson.

It is not that way with the French 75. Rechristenings are not routine. Occasionally a new name is slapped on a derivative drink, or someone plays around with the name to invent, say, a French 95 (which, in fact, exists; it uses bourbon). Very often, though, when the contents change, the name remains French 75. It is quite possibly the most elastic drink on the planet today. If Mencken is correct that 17,864,392,788 different drinks are possible in a typical bar, a full million of them are French 75s. One feels like asking, from the old game show *To Tell the Truth,* in which panelists guessed which contestant really held some exotic occupation, "Will the real French 75 please stand up?"

The best way to think about the French 75 is not to analogize to artist John Constable. His landscapes of the British countryside are beautiful, but scientifically precise. Claude Monet is a better comparator to the cocktail. He painted the same water lilies and haystacks over and over. Each time they changed depending on the atmospherics, time of day, and season.

Several days of random exploration of London bars, when I visited in the summer of 2022, illustrate the French 75's elasticity.

Rules Restaurant has an upstairs bar with rich wood paneling and red carpet. Rules claims to be the oldest restaurant in London, a hangout of Charles Dickens and the assignation-inclined King Edward VII. Sam Porter, a bartender with a perfectly rectangular smile, poured the house French 75, admitted that it was not that interesting, and then produced his own version, which had four drops of Pernod. He served it in a frozen highball glass with ice. London was in the midst of a scorching summer, and this was a good antidote to the heat wave.

Franco's Restaurant claims to be the oldest Italian restaurant in London. The food was excellent; their standard French 75 was not nearly as good as their Negronis. In response to this observation, I was told head bartender Dan Barbuceanu was experimenting with his own French 75, using white balsamic vinegar. Experimenting comes easily to the cheerful bartender, who studied chemistry in his native Romania. The drink was better than it sounds, and when I returned a year later Dan had perfected it into a brilliant summer drink. The final recipe was: Acqueverdi, a floral gin distilled in the Italian alps (25 ml), ten-year-old white balsamic vinegar (5 ml), and three drops of grenadine, topped with Champagne. The drink is garnished with a lemon twist and served in a flute. Dan also stepped out of the box by naming it Franco's 61, after its address, 61 Jermyn Street.

Late one evening, I ducked into the bar at upscale Chutney Mary's on St. James Street. The bartender at the Indian restaurant said he made his French 75 with a brown sugar cube. I scoffed behind my sleeve, only to learn later that "a lump of sugar doused with Angostura" is used in the French-75-like Maharajah's Burra-Peg, which global cocktail chaser Charles Baker said in the 1930s was "to the ordinary Champagne Cocktail what Helen of Troy was to a local shepherd maiden."

This kaleidoscopic variability bespeaks the fluidity of the French 75. It does not tell us how this fluidity came to be. To understand this aspect of L'Affaire des Soixante-Quinze we need to plumb the drink's special attachment to propaganda.

CHAPTER TWO

IT IMPOSES ITSELF ON OUR THOUGHTS

L'Affaire des Quatorze, which so troubled Louis XV, was about one big thing: *opinion publique*. "Public opinion now has, in Europe, a preponderant power against which one cannot resist," said the French writer and court-watcher Louis-Sébastien Mercier. The next king, Louis XVI, found out the hard way. He lost public support and his head.

It subsequently came to pass that those in power,

whether by inheritance or election, learned to shape public opinion to their advantage. In studying the behavior of crowds, the nineteenth-century French sociologist Gustave Le Bon observed, "The power of words is bound up with the images they evoke. . . . Reason and arguments are incapable of combatting certain words and formulas."

Accordingly, when the Great War broke out, it also came to pass:

- That the newly harnessed power of systematic, pervasive propaganda became as much a factor in prosecution of the war as France's powerful new 75 mm artillery piece.

- That the war for French citizens' minds and the powerful cannon directed at the enemy became intertwined.

- And that this combination produced a drink whose name resonated after the guns were moved to French parks to memorialize victory.

CANON DE 75 MM MODÈLE 1897

On a rainy Sunday morning, February 7, 1915, women fanned out across France carrying emblems of the French 75 cannon. Passersby dropped coins in baskets hanging around the women's necks and plucked out one of the various medals, some simple and some elaborate, suspended from a red, white, and blue ribbon, the colors of the French flag. "No one would have dared to continue walking with an undecorated buttonhole," a French artilleryman recalled. Some patriots did not stop at acquiring one medal. They wanted one of each type.

Twenty-two million medals ended up in buttonholes that day. The coins donated for them piled up to nearly 5.5 million francs. The Touring Club of France, which organized the fund drive, used the money to send care packages to men at the front. But La Journée du 75 also paid a large emotional dividend. "The glorification of the 75 gave our soldiers a sense of well-being. It also created a great feeling of fraternal union among all French people,"

The French 75 medal. (Photo by Sam Gregory Anselmo)

the artilleryman said in a book he ostensibly wrote. *Notre 75: Une Merveille du Génie Français* (*Our 75: A Marvel of French Ingenuity*) was beautifully produced with a pop-up representation of the gun on a cardboard flyleaf endsheet. Another expression of propaganda, it appeared shortly after the event.

The creation story of the marvelous cannon added to its patriotic mystique. Work on the gun began in secret following France's humiliating defeat in the Franco-Prussian War of 1870–71. The French hid the funding for the project and put out disinformation to disguise the work. One ruse may have led to the infamous Dreyfus Affair. L'Affaire, as it became known, involved a young officer named Alfred Dreyfus, who was wrongly convicted of treason in 1895 for passing artillery secrets to the Germans—secrets that may have been intended to divert the Germans' attention from the French 75. The details would take too long to relate in a book that is about something else. The point is that Dreyfus, a convenient scapegoat because he was haughty and Jewish, was possibly framed to hide the identity of a double agent and the goal of the disinformation plot.

The hyper-secret military did not acknowledge the existence of their new artillery piece until Bastille Day 1899, two years after it went into mass production. Even then, details on the gun remained classified. The gun was designed so that artillerymen could blow up classified components of the weapon if the enemy was about to overrun their position.

The Canon de 75 mm Modèle 1897 gave the French an advantage when the war broke out. It was the first modern field gun. Unlike its predecessors, whose entire structure lurched backward when a round was fired, only the 75's barrel recoiled; the carriage holding the barrel stayed put. Because the gunners did not have to reposition the carriage for the next shot, they could rapidly reload. The gun fired up to thirty rounds a minute. Another outstanding feature was the 75's ability to hit targets by indirect fire. As historian David Stevenson summed up, the 75 delivered "intense and accurate surprise bombardment from a hidden position."

The 75 helped stop the German advance toward Paris in the first weeks of the war. Afterward, when belligerents

Pop-up illustration from the propaganda book *Notre 75*, depicting the artillery piece that was instrumental to the Allied success in the First World War. (Photo by Sam Gregory Anselmo)

settled in to protracted trench warfare, artillery took on greater importance than in the past. In the Franco-Prussian War the ratio of artillery pieces to soldiers was 1:350; in the latter part of the Great War, the ratio was 1:60. The steady artillery bombardment kept the opposing sides in their trenches. If an attack was to be made, hours of shelling beforehand cleared obstacles and demoralized the enemy.

The French 75 shell. (National WWI Museum and Memorial)

"There are no words between the covers of the dictionary which can convey any adequate idea of what one of these great artillery actions is like," war correspondent E. Alexander Powell wrote. So intense was the experience that a new pair of words was coined: Shell Shock.

Powell was one of the few American journalists to get to the front lines in the early stages of the war. The Allies facilitated the trip because of its propaganda value. In letters to his parents, Powell acknowledged he wanted to advertise "the wonderful work the French are accomplishing." His glorification focused on the role of artillery and especially on the contribution of the 75. In one of his quickly written Great War books, *Vive la France!*, published in 1915, the year the French 75 cocktail appeared, Powell observed, "The guns to which the French owe their success in Champagne, the guns which may well prove the deciding factor in this war, are not the cumbersome siege pieces or the mammoth naval cannon, but the mobile, quick-firing, never-tiring, hard-hitting, 'seventy-fives,' whose fire, the Germans resentfully exclaim, is not deadly but murderous."

The number of 75s grew from four thousand at the start of the conflict to twelve thousand by its end. Because the United States was ill-prepared for the war, the American Expeditionary Forces under General John Pershing acquired two thousand 75s from the French. Future president Harry Truman commanded a 75 mm field artillery battery. One of his soldiers wrote of "the destruction that had been wrought by our guns. It looked like humans, dirt, rock, trees and steel had been turned up by one plow."

A good deal of war reporting had the same mission as shrill bagpipes on the battlefield—to encourage people to lose reason and throw themselves into the fight. The 75 gun provided inspirational material, such as this one-liner in the *New Orleans Herald:* "American gunners are teaching those French 75s to 'talk United States to the Germans.'" The first issue of the British *War Illustrated* reported, "The French '75s' have so scared German gunners that their officers chain them to their guns in order to hold them in the firing line." Two months later the magazine ran a full page of photos on the cannon with an image of the Journée du

75 medal. The patriotic publisher of the *War Illustrated* was awarded a peerage.

The blazing 75 cannon was a tangible symbol of strength, glory, and hope. When promoting the La Journée du 75 fund-raising campaign in February 1915, *Les Annales* exhorted, "Why is the hero of this day the 75 gun? Because, from the beginning of hostilities, this admirable defender gave us hope. Because it was there, as was French valor. Because it stands for, in the eyes of the whole world, the approaching victory. Give on February 7—and there will be joy in the trenches."

FROM *CANON* TO COCKTAIL

The February 7 La Journée du 75 was so successful that it was repeated. As *la journée* turned into *l'année,* the gun became a bountiful source of related propaganda.

Songs were written about the gun. The poem "Our 75" proclaimed, "It imposes itself on our thoughts / The name of the glorious cannon." Images of the gun appeared on romantic postcards ("L'Artillerie de L'Amour") and on postcards the military gave to servicemen to write home from the front. The gun was emblazoned on posters; clocks and watches; board games; pens and sculpted inkwells; cigarette papers, cigarette cases, and cigarette lighters; plates, spoons, and coffee mugs; ersatz coffee, wines, and chocolates; spools of cotton thread; plaques; handkerchiefs, decorative boxes; padlocks; rings. This patriotism was tinged with commercial opportunism. Ersatz coffee looked more enticing if it bore the name 75 and was sipped from a 75 mug. But commercial marketing played into the hands of government propagandists, for it further imposed the glories of the gun on the thoughts of Frenchwomen and Frenchmen.

At some point in 1915, a cocktail appeared with the 75 appellation appended to it. It was one of the more apt gun-inspired christenings. The first recorded version with applejack and gin was powerful like the gun. Imbibing it was simultaneously a ready relief from the grim trenches and an act of patriotism. The front lines were only ninety minutes from Paris. An Allied officer on leave could make a beeline to an Opéra district bar to ease his nerves while paying homage to the guns that only hours before thundered protectively around him.

In this respect the French 75 was a singular expression of sympathy for the Allied cause. The only rival cocktail was the Sidecar. Some said an army captain invented it and named it for the seat attachment to his military motorcycle. But the war connection was vague and the name too anodyne to provoke a salute. That was not the case with the French 75.

The 75 cannon and the 75 cocktail were a symbiotic duo. It is more than coincidence that Powell introduced the drink to New York columnist O. O. McIntyre when he was in town promoting a French propaganda film. The drink propagandized the war; the war advertised the cocktail.

So heady was the link between the cocktail and the gun that romanticism set in. One fantastic story was told by humorist Jean Shepherd. In an irritatingly bizarre 1969 radio program, Shepherd claimed the French 75 could be "traced to one person," Raoul Lufbery, who made it with

Cognac and not apple brandy. Lufbery was a member of the Lafayette Escadrille, a unit largely made up of American volunteer fighter pilots who drank French 75s to salute fallen comrades.

The problem with this tale is the Lafayette Escadrille took to the sky in 1916, months after the drink was mentioned in the press. Others have imagined French pilots or British soldiers drank the cocktails out of a 75 mm brass casing or that French soldiers quaffed them before going into battle. Powell, who left journalism to become an intelligence officer on Pershing's staff, reported in another one of his war books, "I have never seen spirits of any kind in use in the zone of operations." His efforts to debunk canards about tipsy fighting Frenchmen met with little success. Propaganda is intoxicating.

This was only the beginning. After the war, sloppiness with facts, the creation of pure fiction, and myth making carried on as bartenders reimagined the drink with parallel vigor. Before reprising that history, we visit the first watering holes associated with L'Affaire des Soixante-Quinze.

CHAPTER THREE

SOME BARS AND SOME BARTENDERS

Fixing a date for the first French 75 is like fixing the date for the first lovers' kiss. French 75-like cocktails happened, naturally, on multiple occasions in multiple places, starting perhaps with Adam and Eve's first-kiss innocence in John Milton's Paradise, where "for drink the Grape / She crushes, inoffensive moust, and meathes / From many a berrie, and from sweet kernels prest."

Certainly, Frenchwomen and Frenchmen sipped Champagne-and-brandy precursors to the French 75. The brandy could have been Calvados, Armagnac, or Cognac,

IN SEARCH OF
the FRENCH
75

LONDON
BUCK'S CLUB
THE SAVOY

PARIS
HARRY'S
NEW YORK BAR

AURORA
FRENCH 75 LOUNGE

WASHINGTON, DC
FOUNTAIN INN

NEW ORLEANS
ARNAUD'S

SINGAPORE
THE ATLAS

depending on where in France they lived. The British, too, had antecedents to the French 75. In his 1872 *Narrative of a Voyage Round the World,* Admiral Edward Belcher noted, "Captain Bening made us a Champagne Cocktail. Half a tumbler of Champagne, a little brandy, a little bitters, a little sugar." When bedding down in Boston's Parker House, Charles Dickens asked for a Champagne cup made with a British drinking staple, gin.

The often-embellished story of the drink's transition from these informal beginnings to a cocktail named French 75 is attached to three famed "American bars" in Europe. The first is on Clifford Street in London's Mayfair district. Buck's Club bar is occasionally said to be the nursery of the French 75. When I visited—to give you an inkling of what is to come—the bartender served the Buck's Fizz.

BUCK'S CLUB

Buck's Club is not the oldest private club in London. Many had flourished for centuries before the haunt opened its doors in 1919. Buck's competes with these older clubs by having quickly stocked its storehouse of lore. The individual who contributed more than any other to its fame was comic author P. G. Wodehouse. He was not a member but visited often. He mentioned the club by its real name in his amusing novels and as a setting for the Drones Club, a hangout for upper-class ne'er-do-wells, who, like bees of the same name, spend their days doing nothing worthwhile. Crises arise in Wodehouse's stories when a feverish member—Wodehouse calls the members Eggs—is smitten by a young woman whom he clumsily pursues until her father, such as the sixth Earl of Wivelscome, unmasks him as a twit.

One story starts this way:

The annual smoking-concert of the Drones Club had just come to an end, and it was the unanimous verdict of the little group assembled in the bar for a last quick one that the gem of the evening had been item number six on the programme, the knockabout cross-talk act of Cyril ("Barmy") Fotheringay-Phipps and Reginald ("Pongo") Twistleton-

Twistleton. Both Cyril, in the red beard, and Reginald, in the more effective green whiskers, had shown themselves, it was agreed, at the very peak of their form. . . . "In fact," said an Egg, "it struck me that they were even better than last year. Their art seemed to have deepened somehow."

Buck's began as a retreat for military officers who fought in the Great War. It has eschewed pretense, intellectual or otherwise. Its library is small. In keeping with the interests of its chief founder and impresario until his death in 1966, Captain Herbert John Buckmaster of the Royal Horse Guards, the all-male membership is inclined to sports. Buckmaster was an avid gambler at the racetrack.

Today the club has its own polo team, and members engage in late-night whiffle ball cricket matches in the second-floor bar. This is quite unlike, say, the Carlton Club. That stuffier enclave is heavily loaded with Tory politicians in drab suits who jostle around the downstairs bar like parched wildebeests at a Serengeti waterhole. Not that drinking is foreign to Buck's. This, too, is part of its reputation. The club's first bartender, Malachy "Pat" McGarry,

No French 75s are served on the Long Bar in Buck's Club, but they surely were in the past. The painting over the fireplace mantel is of the club's founder, Captain Herbert John Buckmaster of the Royal Horse Guards. [Courtesy of Buck's Club]

appeared in Wodehouse stories under his real name, something that was unusual for a Wodehouse character.

McGarry presided at the American Bar, so named by Buckmaster because of the many American friends he had accumulated in the trenches and in sports. This according to the club secretary, Major Rupert Lendrum. By way of amplification on the Major's explanation for the name, many British cocktail bars called themselves "American" around this time to indicate that they served cocktails, which were identified with the United States. This marked a difference with British bars that served a spirit such as Scotch with water, ice, or tonic. Similarly, the French used the name *bar américain* to denote bars specializing in cocktails.

The battered lumber that McGarry once stood behind is referred to as the Long Bar. This is a misnomer. It does not measure more than five yards. Its notability lies in the fact that it is the first bar of any kind in a gentlemen's club, also according to the Major. Hitherto, members sat in lounges where drinks were served to them. Buck's trailblazing approach to getting drunk standing up is now standard in London clubs.

McGarry, too, is considered a trailblazer. Like the hall porter Hooper, he came to the club with military credentials. He served in the Irish Guards in World War I. Buckmaster considered him "the greatest bar man of all time." He is best known for creating the club's signature drink, the Buck's Fizz. This is made of Champagne, orange juice, and other ingredients that the club keeps secret. One of his other legendary creations is the French 75.

This legend had not reached the ears of Major Lendrum. When I asked to visit, he "express[ed] some surprise." "To be honest," he said, "I have not heard of any connection between the French 75 and Buck's Club. I have been here fifteen years and not once has it been mentioned." He could not see how a visit would be worth my while. There also was the distraction of the Queen's platinum jubilee celebration. The club mounted its own festivities, in which the Major had a special interest. In addition to fourteen years in the military, he had been Prince Charles's senior equerry for several years. On the Internet one can view a portrait of the Major in a scarlet uniform with giant gold epaulettes weighing down his shoulders.

He describes himself as having been in the "Champagne business" for a time.

I pressed my case for admittance by referring to the many articles that tied the cocktail to the American Bar. In due course the Major greeted me in the lounge on the second floor. He was dressed in an elegant navy-blue suit seemingly tailored on Saville Row, just around the corner, and directly guided me to the adjacent Long Bar, where Peter the bartender had prepared a Buck's Fizz. Pat McGarry's invention gleamed with neon apricot hues. The drink tasted as good as it looked. While I sipped, I questioned the bartender.

Had he made a French 75 in the last month?

"No."

In the last year?

"No."

Ever?

"No."

Did he know how to make one?

"I've never made one."

How long had he been at the club?

"Six years."

Quod erat demonstrandum! The Major's faintly bemused countenance showed that he rested his case! Buck's Club plus the French 75: They add up to zero. No connection as far as anyone knows. Buck's Fizz is by far the most popular drink. Lendrum keeps close track. The French 75 was not among the list of drinks on offer in the American Bar, nor was he aware that anyone, ever, had asked for one. When I offered some intriguing snippets of L'Affaire des Soixante-Quinze, the Major politely showed no interest.

To give the Major his due, the McGarry plus French 75 origin legend is myth. The reader who is paying attention to what was said earlier in this book knows the French 75 could not have been invented at Buck's. The cocktail existed during the war, and the club did not.

Contrary to the Major's contention otherwise, however, Buck's Club is not a dry hole insofar as the French 75 is concerned. Buck's sloshes with relevancy.

To start with, the club illustrates how much fiction swirls around the drink. Statements about the club and the French 75 often run like this one from *Feast Magazine,*

Harry McElhone, who perfected the absinthe-laced French 75, is one of the twentieth century's greatest bartenders, and his book a classic.

which argued that a "likely origin" of the cocktail "resides in the pages of Harry MacElhone's recipe book, *Harry's ABC of Mixing Cocktails,* first published in 1919. MacElhone gave credit to Pat McGarry of Buck's Club in London. As is the origin of many, many cocktails, he took a simple recipe, modified it, and gave it a new name. He took a Tom Collins recipe that called for gin, lemon juice, sugar, and club soda and replaced the soda with Champagne. Allegedly the Champagne is where the 'French' part comes into play; it's that simple."

It's *not* that simple. This paragraph is riddled with errors. The French 75 is not called *French* because of the Champagne, and the recipe that *Feast Magazine* provides is not the one in the first *ABC of Mixing Cocktails.* Nor did McElhone credit McGarry for the French 75. It credited him for the "Side-Car," writing next to it, "Recipe by

MacGarry [sic], the popular bar-tender at Buck's Club, London." Nor did Harry spell his name as MacElhone. He wrote it as McElhone. Harry's descendants changed the spelling. The misspelling of McGarry's name is partly McElhone's fault. It appeared that way in his *ABC of Mixing Cocktails.*

Finally, McElhone's book did not appear in 1919. The 1919 publishing date is a common error. The MacElhones repeat it all the time. Cocktail professor David Wondrich used the 1919 date in an email to me. When I asked about it, he replied, "Sorry—I'm so used to thinking of it in bartenders' shorthand, where the first edition is generally referred to as that." He believes the book appeared in December 1922, the first date for it in the *English Catalogue of Books.* A second edition appeared early the next year.

How could a famous book published in 1922 be said, for decades, to have been published in 1919? How is it that a knowledgeable bartender like Sam Porter at Rules can go on at length as to whether credit for the drink should belong to Harry or Pat? (He says his "bartender's intuition" tells him that it is Harry.) Part of the problem is that the first edition of Harry McElhone's book did not have a date on it, and the same was true for other editions. But this is minor compared to the larger truth, mentioned earlier: Cocktail culture is not rigid. It's more like a guy draped over a bar while teetering on a stool.

But hold on. L'Affaire des Soixante-Quinze is not closed at this point insofar as Buck's Club is concerned. It is one thing to say the cocktail's invention at the club is emblematically mythical, and quite another to say the early history of the drink and of the club do not intersect in any tangible way. The McElhone-McGarry connection in the *Feast* article is a clue.

When cocktails became a thing in Europe, bartenders who could make them were in demand. Many were itinerant. They moved from bar to bar, much as people in Silicon Valley move from one high tech firm to another, taking their expertise and ideas with them. This cross pollination led to the diffusion of new cocktails.

McElhone was particularly peripatetic. The Dundee-born Scotsman learned his trade in New York and London, and on the Riviera and in Paris. A couple of years after the war broke out, he enlisted in the Royal Naval Air Service, which assigned him to patrols of the Belgium ports. His military service made him a good candidate to join McGarry at Buck's, which he did when the club opened in 1919.

Club records are sparse. During Buckmaster's time minutes were not kept of meetings. The few papers the club did save were mostly lost during World War II when a German bomb "brought down one or two lovely old ceilings, split some walls and shattered our roof," Buckmaster recalled years later. McGarry carried on the next day serving drinks. His heroic service notwithstanding, the only image of him that survives is a thumbnail sketch on a piece of paper that also depicts other men at the club. It is framed on a wall in the bar.

But if we don't have old cocktail menus or photos of McGarry at work, we can be confident that members bellied up to the bar with a French 75 in mind. They were military men who were in France during the recent war; most if not all were exposed to the popular drink; and Harry McElhone, who certainly was aware of the drink in Paris, if not elsewhere, was standing there at the Long Bar to serve them. Of course, he taught his friend Pat how to mix the cocktail if he didn't already know.

McElhone moved on to other local bars and made a hit at Ciro's American Bar in London, where high society danced, dined, and imbibed French 75s in elegant surroundings. He crossed the English Channel to helm the bar at Ciro's outpost in Deauville, a seaside tourist mecca in Normandy. It was around this time he wrote *"Harry" of Ciro's ABC of Mixing Cocktails,* as the book was initially titled.

Finally, McElhone bought his own place in Paris, the New York Bar, where he had briefly worked during the war. This was in the Opéra quarter, a fecund cocktail sector awash with French 75s. Harry made the French 75 one of his signature drinks.

The Major won't be reviving the French 75 in his precincts any time soon. When I later asked him if any older members might remember having the cocktail at the Long Bar, he laconically replied they did not. The Major is a guardian of the remembered narrative. As he told the *Financial Times,* he doesn't fancy changing policy to admit women as members, given his disinterest in discussing "handbags or shoes." What excited the Major, when we met, was the possibility of acquiring a collection of antique Wodehouse books for the club's library. If members read these, they will be reminded of "McGarry, the chappie behind the bar," but nowhere on the premises will they get the full story of all the cocktails he made.

HARRY'S NEW YORK BAR

I hoped to find Franz Arthur MacElhone at his great-grandfather's bar around noon, the normal opening time. The door was locked. When I knocked, he let me in. Passing through the battered swinging batwing doors, I could see the long, narrow, well-used barroom. At the far end of the scuffed mahogany, a television crew was setting up to do an interview with Laurent Giraud, the maître de bar and a natural for the medium. "It's never about us," Giraud said self-deprecatingly when the camera began to roll. "It's about the bar and its traditions."

Harry's original French 75. (Photo by Sam Gregory Anselmo)

If Harry's New York Bar were a cocktail, it would be a pony of alcohol, a jigger of history, and a double shot of hype. After Harry McElhone bought the New York Bar on 5 Rue Daunou in 1923 and added his name to the sign on the glass front window, he made it a regular stop for expatriate Americans and for Parisians who wanted to hang around expatriate Americans, many of whom were celebrities. To-day tourists flock to the bar so they can say they have had "the experience," Franz Arthur says. The bartenders wear the same short white bar jackets and aprons, and black ties that Harry prescribed.

The cluttered wood-paneled walls drip with memora-bilia that qualify by time-in-service as relics: a horseshoe from the great racehorse Man o' War, hockey sticks from the Finnish national hockey team, the boxing gloves of Primo Carnera (the ashes of a loyal patron are in one of the gloves, according to Giraud), yellowed articles about Harry's bar, fading photos of patrons, and scores of Ameri-can college pennants. One afternoon, while I sat at the bar, a mostly teetotaling middle-aged woman from Oklahoma dropped in to find her state university colors.

Laurent Giraud exemplifies the best traditions of Harry McElhone's cocktail emporium. (Photo by author)

The bar's mere existence is a form of self-promotion. Journalists flock there for an easy story—provided they don't feel a need to talk to Franz Arthur.

Franz Arthur had not responded to my emails or returned my phone calls. When we met, he mumbled something unconvincing about annoying calls from lawyers.

The attitude was, if someone wants to talk to me, let them figure out a way. I found a way thanks to one of his bartenders, who tipped me off that he might be coming up from Cannes, where he lives and has another Harry's. Franz Arthur took me to the back of the bar and sat down among the red leather benches.

How many French 75s, I asked, did the bar serve on a typical day?

"Seventy-five."

I looked puzzled.

He continued, "That's my sense of humor."

The real answer, Franz Arthur said, is that 9,000–10,000 French 75s are served each year. It is second to the 13,000 Bloody Marys that cross the bar. The MacElhone family and others say the bar was the Garden of Eden for the Bloody Mary before Harry acquired it. Harry is supposed to have invented the White Lady and Monkey Gland.

Harry's ABC of Mixing Cocktails, as it is now commonly called, was the second cocktail book to publish a recipe for the "75" Cocktail. The first was Robert Vermeire's *Cocktails: How to Mix Them.* It debuted earlier in 1922 and used the same name for the drink, suggesting that was the standard at the time. Both recipes were close to the French 75 reported in 1915, which the reader will recall had gin, grenadine, lemon juice, and applejack. Distilled applejack was treated synonymously with apple brandy and Calvados. Both Vermeire's and McElhone's recipes called for Calvados. The difference was McElhone substituted absinthe for the lemon juice. It is fair to say he was the Thomas Alva Edison of the absinthe French 75.

Vermeire, a Belgium bartender with wide European experience, was highly respected, but he never had a bar to rival Harry's, one of the most famous in the world. Nor did Vermeire's cocktail book go through as many editions as Harry's, which also helped make the latter better known today. Be that as it may, both are classics and both popularized Calvados-driven French 75 recipes. Their books appeared in French-, Spanish-, and English-language bar guides published as far away as Saigon.

Vermeire and McElhone were, of course, only solidifying a cocktail that already had taken hold in Paris. One candidate for launching the drink was, as *Sphere* reported in 1916, "the mixer of the American bar at Ciro's," which was situated across the street from Harry's. But the more likely individual for this honor was a man whose bar was around the corner on Rue Volney. The "literature" supporting this conclusion is Vermeire's book, which notes that "Henry of Henry's bar fame" introduced the cocktail to Paris during the war. Henry probably made his French 75 the way Vermeire did.

In the sketchy annals of the early French 75, Henry Tépé stands out. He was the first bartender to be mentioned by name in connection with the cocktail. The origin of Henry's Bar said a lot about its namesake. While presiding at the Chatham Hotel bar, his "cheery disposition and attention to work" made such a good impression that an American patron, a Southern colonel who fought in the American Civil War, staked him to his own saloon in 1890. Henry's was called the second oldest American bar in Europe, Chatham's being first. "Square Henry," as he came to be known, took care of the colonel when he ran out of money, and he was remembered for his kindnesses to others. American ambulance unit drivers and American aviators were known to frequent his bar during the war.

Tépé's tragic death a few months before the conflict ended in 1918 made news in the United States. The war was acutely painful since he was German-born. His mind slipped to the point that he forgot to put the day's proceeds in the safe. "Ill health and brooding," reported a sympathetic *New York Sun* correspondent, led Tépé to jump out of a second-story window.

Henry's was close to Harry's in significance as well as proximity. It was Harry's before Harry's was Harry's, albeit a trifle more sedate. American foreign correspondent Wythe Williams called it "the gathering place for Americans comparable to the Savoy in London and the Adlon in Berlin." Harry, Williams added, made his bar "the most famous drink emporium in the world outside the United States." Harry shut down the bar when the Germans occupied Paris in World War II. He reopened afterward.

The prehistory of Harry's New York Bar is a snarled mess. "Historians" who frequented it were having too good a time to keep good notes, and McElhone's descendants have not cared much more than patrons. But, to be fair, a teetotaler would have difficulty dividing the fiction from the truth about jockey Tod Sloan. Sloan was a high-rolling, frequently-in-debt husband to actresses, and inventor of the monkey crouch riding position in horse racing. He became involved with the New York Bar, which opened in 1911, but that involvement is subject to widely different stories.

A *New York Times* correspondent, who shared the *Sun's* view that Parisian bars were newsworthy, reported in March 1914 that Sloan bought the New York Bar from another jockey, Milton Henry. A different version comes from playwright and journalist Basil Woon, author of *The Paris That's Not in the Guidebooks* (1931). Woon said that Henry's wife sold it to someone involved with German delicatessens in London and that the new owner hired Sloan as manager.

Harry McElhone's descendants wrote a book, *Harry's Bar,* to celebrate the centennial of the bar. This history claims Sloan started the bar in 1911 and that it was he who arranged with a partner to transport the wooden guts of a New York saloon to the Rue Daunou. According to the MacElhone family, Sloan hired Harry for a short stint after the bar was opened.

Franz Arthur is impatient with attempts to clarify these *Rashomon*-like recollections. "I sometimes feel lost in the flow of questions that I have very often on loads of dates and details we no longer have data for." As a matter of fact, however, we do have "details" that corroborate the *New York Times* story on Sloan's purchase in 1914. One of these is *Tod Sloan,* Sloan's as-told-to autobiography published the following year. The other is a July 1947 article in *Town and Country* magazine that relied on an interview with Harry McElhone. The author, Eckert Goodman, reported that Sloan bought the place around 1914 and hired Harry for a spell because he needed someone to compensate for his feckless management.

In his memoir, Sloan said the purchase was "one of the great mistakes I made." The bar that he singles out as a thriving Paris oasis was Henry Tépé's, "perhaps the best-known man to Americans in Europe." Sloan thought so much of Tépé that he put his photo in his memoir. The jockey died in Los Angeles in 1933. The cause was cirrhosis.

Harry was the P. T. Barnum of bar ballyhoo. His first months as owner were a frenzy of promotional gimmicks. He placed a long-running display ad in the *Paris Herald*. It encouraged visits by American tourists who were bashful about their weak French-language skills. The advertisement gave the phonetic pronunciation of the bar's address: JUST TELL THE TAXI DRIVER SANK ROO DOE NOO. Harry initiated a straw vote among American expatriates for United States presidential elections, which continues to this day, and staged beer-drinking contests. One winner was briefly in the *Guinness Book of World Records*.

Harry created the International Bar Fly society with columnist O. O. McIntyre. It will be recalled that McIntyre was responsible for the first-known English-language reference to the French 75, written when E. Alexander Powell was on his war promotion tour in 1915. McIntyre shared the publicity gene with McElhone. In addition to writing his New York Day-by-Day column, he was on the payroll of the Majestic Hotel, for which he dreamed up publicity stunts. When his column became hugely popular in the 1920s, he made annual pilgrimages to Paris. McIntyre was the IBF's president and McElhone was number two. They deemed Harry's Bar to be the fly's Trap No. 1. Among the founding Bar Flies were Sinclair Lewis, Cole Porter, Jack Dempsey, and Douglas Fairbanks Jr. McIntyre wrote the club song. It consisted largely of the word "buzz."

McElhone dedicated *Bar Flies and Cocktails,* published in Paris in 1927, to McIntyre. This knock-off of his *ABC of Mixing Cocktails* contained a list of charter IBF members, addresses of fly traps around the world, and drawings by illustrator and stage designer Wynn Holcomb. Enjoying the company of journalists, McElhone dedicated one edition of the *ABC of Mixing Cocktails* to Laurence Hills, director of the *Paris Herald* (later *Herald Tribune*).

Scribblers, in turn, treated Harry's bar as a shrine, and he as the patron saint. Novelist Ian Fleming, a heavy drinker, wrote this about James Bond in *For Your Eyes Only:* "If he wanted a solid drink he had it at Harry's Bar, both because of the solidity of the drinks and because, on his first ignorant visit to Paris at the age of sixteen, he had done what

Harry's advertisement in the *Continental Daily Mail* had told him to do and had said to his taxi-driver 'Sank Roo Doe Noo.' That had started one of the memorable evenings of his life, culminating in the loss, almost simultaneous, of his virginity and his note-case."

Eric Hawkins, a former managing editor of the *Paris Herald,* described the wake for a journalist who died when demonstrating he could step out of a second-floor window and survive. "Distinguished international barflies contributed their tears and cheers to the occasion," Hawkins wrote in a memoir, *Hawkins of the Paris Herald,* "including all of Harry's bartenders and Bouboule, the dwarf who opened the door outside the saloon. The wake lasted, properly, until five o'clock in the morning." The next day Harry was outside the church where the funeral was to be held, still drinking with his pals, until he passed out.

Eric Sevareid, who started out with the *Paris Herald* before making his name in broadcast journalism, recalled in *Not So Wild a Dream* that the working style of his colleague Sparrow Robertson meshed with Harry's. "[Robertson] had a fantastic capacity for alcohol and was never, to my knowledge, seen to take in food. He lived only by night, either at Fred Payne's bar in Montmartre or at Harry's New York Bar, and his daily 'sports' column consisted of the exploits and comments of 'my old pal' Fred or Harry or somebody else."

Franz Arthur is tall and lanky, a contrast to his oval-shaped forebear. He does not sit by the front door warmly welcoming customers as Harry did. But when we met, he was a walking-billboard for the bar with his navy-blue blazer displaying the International Bar Fly emblem over the left breast pocket.

Franz Arthur has not tampered with the unprovable, insignificant assertions that encourage credulous holidaymakers to treat Harry's as a UNESCO World Heritage Site. The bar boasts that it is "the oldest cocktail bar in Europe" and the first French bar to serve Coca-Cola. The contraption Harry installed on the mahogany bar in 1933 is supposedly the first hotdog cooker in France. The cooker is the only steady source of food at Harry's apart from the garnish on drinks. (Its French 75s come fruitless.) Franz Arthur insists, against evidence to the contrary, that

Harry's ABC of Mixing Cocktails was published in 1919. When I asked if he had a copy from that date, he replied vaguely about one existing somewhere in Germany.

Franz Arthur also carries on the family tradition of franchising Harry's bars. Besides the one he owns outright in Cannes, he licensed four in Germany, and one that comes and goes in Switzerland. He was planning one for Dubai.

Harry's bar held centennials for the Bloody Mary and the Sidecar. The latter debuted in print in Harry's and Vermeire's cocktail books. The French 75 has not been feted. It does, however, enjoy a perennial advertisement that adds to its popularity. On the wall facing the bar is a French 75 poster with a line that—according to Franz Arthur—author F. Scott Fitzgerald wrote next to the drink in a copy of *Harry's ABC of Mixing Cocktails:* "First, you take a drink, then the drink takes a drink, then the drink takes you."

I did not see the book with Fitzgerald's scribble, which Franz Arthur indicated he has. Fitzgerald borrowed the lines from a Japanese proverb normally written, "First a man takes a drink; then the drink takes a drink; then the drink takes a man." In either case, the syntax of the proverb—which sounds like the mutterings of an inebriated drinker—may have appealed to the often-in-his-cups Fitzgerald. The message is clearly articulated: This is a strong cocktail.

The French 75 served at Harry's today is not Harry's original, as will be discussed later, but it has kept the absinthe. When Laurent Giraud demonstrates how to make the French 75, it is like watching a ballet. He works in accordance with Harry's strict rules in the *ABC of Mixing Cocktails:* "Do all the work in plain view, for there is nothing to conceal, do it as it ought to be done, without any attempt at unusual elaboration."

But when the tourists flocked in on a July 4 evening while I was there, Harry's injunctions were forgotten. Whereas Giraud lightly coats the coupe with absinthe to give a "little hint of freshness," the young bartender on duty dumped absinthe into a shaker. No hints of anything here. The absinthe had a full nelson on the cocktail. Giraud waxes poetic about the coupe. But the city councilman from Pennsylvania who came in for a taste of Harry's tradition was given his French 75 in a brandy glass—something that would never happen at our next stop.

THE SAVOY

In 1927, a slender man, with a high forehead topped off by carefully combed silver hair and wearing a white bar jacket and matching apron, placed a shiny cocktail shaker in a wall and bricked it in. The man was Harry Craddock; the location, in London, was the Savoy Hotel's American Bar, over which he presided; the shaker held Cointreau, gin, and lemon juice. A promotional photo of Craddock, with trowel in hand, was snapped. The cocktail that he was promoting that day was the White Lady, which Craddock considered his signature drink.

In a few years Craddock would make a much bigger splash with a stunning cocktail book that featured a new style of French 75. The cocktail shaker-in-the-wall trick, as well as the White Lady, were minor stunts. The shaker

The French 75 at the Savoy. (Photo by Sam Gregory Anselmo)

Harry Craddock put on a show with this cocktail-in-the-wall trick. But his greatest publicity show was *The Savoy Cocktail Book,* which popularized a new version of the French 75 cocktail. (Courtesy of the Savoy Archive)

has never been found, and the drink is rarely ordered. The book and the French 75 recipe in it became classics.

Bars are theaters in which the performers mix drinks in front of you, as McElhone prescribed. The potential for creative interactions abounds, whether it is wiffle ball cricket at Buck's or presidential election night at Harry's New York

Bar. In this show business, the Savoy had a competitive advantage. It had svelte Harry Craddock, "king of cocktail shakers." And it had—and has—a shimmering stage.

In the story of L'Affaire des Soixante-Quinze, you will not find a swankier hotel than the Savoy. It has luxuriated along the River Thames since 1889. Its bar has as much in common with Harry's Bar as a Rolls Royce dealership does with a used car lot full of Dodge Darts. The man who built it was impresario Richard D'Oyly Carte, who enriched himself by producing Gilbert and Sullivan comic operas. The hotel's innovations included hot and cold running water and newly invented electric lights. It was the first London hotel where respectable ladies could dine in public. Whereas renovation at Harry's is another layer of dust, the Savoy has been updated over and over. It remains a fairyland of happy (well, anyway, they're smiling) and efficient staff. The art deco American Bar gleams with mirrors and a sleek bar top, instead of one made of dark wood.

Harry Craddock was born in the Cotswolds in 1875. Twenty-two years later he immigrated to the United States, where he worked his way up at prestigious bars, became an

The art deco American Bar at the Savoy in 1931, around the time Craddock reinvented the cocktail. (Courtesy of the Savoy Archive)

American citizen, and acquired an American accent. Prohibition in 1920 blew away his job. The Holland House, the grand hotel where he worked at the time, was one of the first in New York to close completely, rooms as well as the bar, according to Daniel Okrent's *Last Call*. Okrent does not mention that Craddock, as the bartender often claimed, made the "last cocktail mixed in New York." It is one of those too-good-to-be-true stories.

Craddock returned to an England where cocktails had acquired, shall we say, a mixed reputation. The quality of preparation was low. Good American-trained bartenders were badly needed. The Savoy snapped up Craddock, who was especially well prepared to serve up the real American experience to expats thirsty for the cocktails they could no longer get at home. The Savoy downplayed that he was British-born and up-played that he was an American citizen. *New York World* reporter Karl K. Kitchen called Craddock "Mr. Manhattan."

Notwithstanding ratification of the women's suffrage amendment to the Constitution, the American bar experience in America did not include women bartenders, and perhaps it was because of this that the Savoy retired its famous barmaid Ada "Coley" Coleman and an equally long-employed female colleague after a 1925 renovation. Craddock became the head barman in Coleman's place.

Craddock was a showman like Richard D'Oyly Carte. As noted in *The Deans of Drink,* he became a cocktail apostle, writing in the *Daily Express,* "One does not drink a cocktail merely to mollify thirst any more than one merely wears clothes to keep warm. The object of a true cocktail, when created by an artist, is that it shall give point and piquancy to that meal of which it is the forerunner." His promotional activities often were of the drink-in-the-wall variety. As with the theater trick of draping a large snake on a ballerina, whose beauty supposedly tamed the drooping reptile, truth was stretched. Craddock did not invent the first cocktail by the name White Lady. Harry McElhone mixed one under that name earlier. But Craddock remade it almost entirely. He rose to the occasion to commemorate special events, for instance, the Leap Year Cocktail, whose date of birth is, according to the Savoy, February 29, 1928. The Savoy avers the cocktail was "responsible for more proposals than any other cocktail that has ever been mixed."

The same year Craddock put the cocktail shaker in the wall, his effigy was put on display in Madame Tussauds' touristy wax museum in London. Celebrity cartoonist Al Hirschfeld captured his likeness in a caricature in the *London Daily Express*. Such was Craddock's fame that his off-duty hobby of fly fishing made its way into the news, along with reports that he undertook a gym workout regime before the high point of the cocktail season.

Craddock and the Savoy reached the pinnacle of promotion in 1930. That year they orchestrated a bar "happening" that became a truly historic event in cocktail history, *The Savoy Cocktail Book*. The Savoy's managing director had the idea for the book. The 750 recipes were Craddock's. The beautifully produced volume presented, as one historian has commented, "a kaleidoscopic view of the era's mixed drinks."

One of those drinks was a reimagined French 75, which Craddock called the French "75" Cocktail. He did not pour in Calvados. Nor did he use grenadine; nor any anise-flavored spirit that might be a turn-off to some palates. His version contained dry gin, lemon juice, and powdered sugar. He finished it with Champagne. The drink was served in a flute with cracked ice. This was a simple cocktail, no garnish. It fit the Savoy, which relentlessly aimed to please every tourist who came in the door. There was nothing about the cocktail to dislike.

Craddock was not the first to propose a French 75 along these lines. American illustrator Norman Hume Anthony, who wrote under the name Judge Jr., in homage to the weekly satirical magazine *Judge* that he edited, included the identical concoction in his 1927 *Here's How!* (To confuse things, a subsequent book, *Here's How Again!*, carried a French 75 made Harry McElhone's way—Calvados, absinthe, etc.—and called it The Tunney, perhaps after the boxing champion.)

Judge Jr. commanded attention, but not to the degree that Harry Craddock did. Judge was a journalist resident in Prohibition America. Craddock was a fecund cocktail inventor resident in *the* Savoy and burnished his reputation even more when he cofounded the United Kingdom Bartenders Guild.

The Savoy Cocktail Book, which was published simultaneously in the United States, became the Bible for cocktail connoisseurs. Although it was impossible to keep bartenders from fiddling with the recipe, they used it as a guide for French 75s. In 1945, in an attempt to establish "UNIFORMITY IN METHODS AND MIXING" (emphasis in the original), the Chicago Bartenders and Beverage Dispensers Union Local No. 278 published *Recipes* with the Savoy's version for the French 75, albeit with two ice cubes in place of the cracked ice the Savoy used. It is not clear when Harry's New York Bar fell into step, but eventually it did. It employs Craddock's gin and Champagne, but retains McElhone's touches: a coupe glass with no ice and a whiff of absinthe.

Harry Craddock's recipes alone do not account for the fame of *The Savoy Cocktail Book.* Susan Scott, the Savoy archivist, is rhapsodic about the book and a purist about its history, as befits a woman who studied classics in the university. When we met in one of the lounges of the Savoy, she sniffed at the idea of calling Craddock the author. He signed the books with such phrases as "with best wishes of the author." But the narrative and witty statements came from real writers, hired by the hotel publicist. One of these freelancers, she says, was Vyvyan Holland, the son of Oscar Wilde. The *bon mots* added to the appeal of the book, as this one for the Rattlesnake Cocktail: "So called because it will either cure Rattlesnake bite, or kill Rattlesnakes, or make you see them." Another appealing feature was Gilbert Rumbold's amusing illustrations. The book has been called "the most stylish drink book ever produced."

In supply-and-demand terms, the book was ideal for the French 75. Craddock supplied the sparkling new French 75. The classy book encouraged people to want it.

The hotel has kept *The Savoy Cocktail Book* continuously in print. New editions have preserved the old recipes and included new ones. The latest edition contains the art and wit of the original. The hotel gives it to clients as a sort of party favor. In addition to enhancing the prestige of the hotel, the book serves as a time capsule. A serious collection of bar books must contain *The Savoy Cocktail Book*.

The Savoy's American Bar has continued to innovate. The current French 75 differs from the one in the Savoy book. Susan Scott and I had one made by Cristian Silenzi, an Italian with a broad smile. The cocktail has the usual sugar syrup, lemon juice, and Champagne, but it does not use dry gin. Silenzi poured botanical Bombay Sapphire gin, which Susan Scott says captures the "green" spirit of the bar. One other change is the addition of a fat, aged, burgundy-colored maraschino cherry, plunked in the narrow bottom of the flute. The drink is topped off with a spray of lemon zest. No ice. For this, one pays about twice as much as at Harry's New York Bar. Whether it is better than Harry's is questionable, but it never comes in a brandy glass.

Craddock left the Savoy in 1938 for the Dorchester Hotel, which had just built a handsome bar. There he put three drinks in the wall, one of which was his White Lady. He later moved to Brown's Hotel. After that he dropped out of sight, living on National Assistance in an old people's home. He died in 1963 and, sadly, lies in a common grave.

When we met at the Savoy, Susan Scott wondered how the French 75 has remained so popular for so long. *The*

Savoy Cocktail Book, she said, has many terrific recipes among its hundreds of entries. One cocktail enthusiast, an elderly gentleman who cherished a copy of the book he inherited from his father, wrote her that he tried all the recipes and that the Mah-Jong Cocktail was his favorite. Why hasn't the Mah-Jong maintained the popularity it had during Prohibition but the French 75 has?

One reason is that the Mah-Jong was liquor + liquor + liquor, that is, Cointreau, gin, and rum. That cocktail, like Harry McElhone's early French 75 with gin and Calvados, is strong. Lighter, fresher drinks are more in fashion these days. As Scott wrote to me after we drank the updated green version at the Savoy, "I am truly astonished by how many variants there are, but whatever it was that I drank in the American Bar was perfectly delicious."

The French 75 is a superb drink that has been taught new tricks to keep up with the times. But that is not the only reason for its long run of stardom, as we are about to find out.

CHAPTER FOUR

COCKTAIL *REPARTIE*

During the years McGarry, McElhone, and Craddock, as well as Vermeire and Judge Jr., were mixing French 75s, they kept alive the memory of the drink's attachment to the artillery cannon. "The cocktail," Robert Vermeire wrote next to the recipe in his *Cocktails: How to Mix Them,* "was very well appreciated in Paris during the war. It has been called after the famous light French field gun." More than a decade after the war Harry McElhone's book reminded readers the drink was named "after the French light field gun." Judge Jr.'s *Here's How* joked, "This drink is really what won the War for the Allies."

Whereas the earlier versions deserved to be likened to an artillery piece based on their power, the later ones were not so strong, which was also in a way fitting. For inevitably, the urge to toast victory in the Great War gradually faded. New wars came along, and the French 75 cannon was no longer a commanding presence on those new battlefields. It was only fired for ceremonial salutes. The inkwells with statues of the gun became war memorabilia, as did the medals and all the rest—all, that is, but the cocktail.

New recipes were invented, propelled forward less by the war than by something else. The French 75 continued to impose itself on the public's thoughts because of the mellifluousness of its name.

THE FRENCH 75
GOES TO THE MOVIES

Three men walk into a bar.

"Gimme a Phlegm Cutter," says one of them.

"Make mine a Fuzzy Navel," the second man says.

"A French 75, please," says the last man.

Which of these individuals would you want to prepare your taxes, lead you on an expedition up the Amazon River, act as your personal shopper for a new suit of clothes, or marry someone in your immediate family?

A Phlegm Cutter would make for a good line in a W. C. Fields movie. It's easier to imagine who would not order a Fuzzy Navel than who would. But the French 75 . . . there is a name to conjure with.

One did not need to be reminded of the cocktail's battlefield fame to be drawn to it. There was no embarrassment in ordering a French 75. It spoke of élan and something else. For onlookers unaware of the military root of the name, the cocktail carried an air of enigmatic elitism. Its name must have meaning, but what was it? The individual who ordered a French 75 knew something they did not know. A Cosmopolitan cocktail did not make you cosmopolitan. It was a step up from rum and coke. A gin fizz made you a good fellow, fun to have along for the ride. The Stinkibus, a drink that H. L. Mencken tied to the Gothic Age of American drinking, made you weird. A French 75 made you an enviable object of interest, an insider.

The French 75 suggested martial glory, glamour, and mystery, and you could play amusing tricks with it. The French 75 lent itself to witticisms in cocktail recipe books. "Hits with remarkable precision," Vyvyan Holland quipped in *The Savoy Cocktail Book.* It lent itself to poster art, which came alive in France around the time the cannon and the drink were invented. Hence the poster at Harry's New York Bar with F. Scott Fitzgerald's quote about the drink. And it lent itself to the silver screen, another new art form that called for clever dialogue.

In the MGM film *Riptide* (1934), the French 75 appeared in a setting as bright and shiny as the Savoy's American Bar. Lady Mary Rexford (Norma Shearer) has just been shunned by her husband, Lord Rexford (Herbert Marshall), because he mistakenly thinks she has had a fling with Tommie Trent (Robert Montgomery), an old playboy flame who wishes the fire was still burning. Morose Mary and the disappointed Tommie, both dressed in evening clothes, go to the bar.

> *Tommie:* Have a drink?
> *Mary:* Love to!
> *Tommie:* Name it!
> *Mary:* Eh, French 75.
> *Tommie:* Same here. French 75. Boom!
> *Mary (gloomily):* Boom yourself! And everyone else.
> *Tommie:* That a girl.

A poster for the film shows Mary and Tommie toasting each other with French 75s.

John Wayne costarred twice with a French 75. The Cold War movie *Jet Pilot* (1957) is not worth much space here other than to mention our hero says the downside to defecting to Russia is having to make a French 75 with vodka. In *A Man Betrayed* (1941), which is slightly better, the cocktail is a device to show the lack of sophistication of Lynn Hollister (Wayne), an earnest young lawyer from a small town. The French 75's cameo occurs in a smoky bar. Hollister sits across from elegant Sabra Cameron (Frances Dee), with whom he will presently fall in love while exposing her corrupt politician father. Sabra orders a French 75 and asks Lynn if he has ever had one.

> *Lynn:* Nope, but I shot one on our courthouse lawn. Gave me an awful kick.
>
> *Sabra:* Same idea.
>
> *Waiter* (*to Lynn*)*:* What's your pleasure?
>
> *Lynn:* Throwing eggs in an electric fan. But that's out of season, so just give me a cup of coffee.

The most memorable French 75 performance harkens back to its war roots. The setting is Vichy-controlled Casablanca. A nameless German officer and lovely Yvonne (French actress Madeleine Lebeau) walk into Rick's Café Américain. Yvonne's manic exuberance is due to getting drunk after being jilted by Rick (Humphrey Bogart, as if anyone reading this book would not know that). The German, happy that France is in the hands of the Germans, calls for French 75s. Yvonne sweeps her arm along the bar.

"Put up a whole row of them," she tells the bartender.

"We will begin with two," the German commands.

Later German officers gather around a piano to sing "Die Wacht am Rhein," a patriotic song rooted in Franco-German enmity. Yvonne stares despondently into her drink. When the orchestra breaks in with the "Marseillaise," she jumps to her feet and, tears glistening, sings with the rest of the French customers, who drown out the Germans. "Vive La France!" she shouts, "Vive la démocratie!"

Casablanca, released in late 1942 to take advantage of the publicity around the Allied invasion of North Africa, is as much a propaganda movie as the 1915 "fighting in France" film E. Alexander Powell promoted in New York, only it won a slew of Academy Awards, including for the screenplay.

FAMOUS FOR BEING FAMOUS

The French 75 cocktail became famous for being famous, to borrow historian Daniel Boorstin's phrase about the rise of pseudo-events. A comparison that comes to mind is Paul Newman–branded salad dressing, popcorn, and pet food. Young people who see rows upon rows of "Newman's Own" in the grocery store sometimes are unaware of what really made him famous. "He was an actor, too?" one once asked me.

"French 75" could be applied like a coat of paint to anything one wanted to adorn. (Literally, there are French 75 clothing stores in Cyprus and elsewhere.) You didn't have to like the drink particularly. You simply had to like the sound of the name or the images the name brought to mind.

This was driven home to me one day when I was googling the phrase *French 75*. To my amazement I found myself looking wide-eyed at the French 75 Lounge and Art Gallery in, of all places, Aurora, Illinois, a town along the Fox River west of Chicago. The bar is on Galena Boulevard, down the street from where my father had a laundromat.

Paris is the City of Light and Aurora is the City of Lights. In both cases, they had lots of streetlights ahead of their time. The comparison ends there. My initial venture in (underage) drinking was a reflection of local preferences. I was a hod carrier for a fly-by-night bricklaying company. Before work we drank beers in a dive that opened at 7 a.m. The bibacious masons introduced me to Scotch and milk after work. I never heard one of them, or any of my parents' friends, mention the French 75 cocktail.

I called Braden Smith, who owns the French 75 Lounge and Art Gallery with his artist mother, Hope Ashworth. They did not choose the name French 75 out of a preference for the drink or the illustrious history of the cannon. Braden's favorite drink is the Penicillin, which has Scotch and honey. They chose "French 75" because of the sentiment it conveyed. "It was a way to give a little insight into what we are," Braden said, "a French salon–style art gallery that serves craft cocktails." Customers can buy the art on the walls and order from a list of cocktails that includes the three different styles of French 75s he serves to justify the lounge's name.

Here lies another clue to L'Affaire des Soixante-Quinze. Whereas many modified drinks get new monikers, the French 75 carries on in new iterations because the name is now, as it originally was, exciting.

For the ultimate expression of the French 75's ability to propagandize itself, we turn southward. In New Orleans's French Quarter, the appeal of the words "French 75" prompted the creation of a bar by that name, which in turn contributed to the national renaissance of the cocktail.

CHAPTER FIVE

THE NEW ORLEANS RENAISSANCE

Prohibition was a misnomer. The flouting of the Noble Experiment's laws was widespread and brazen.

Booze could be found in underground speakeasies, backyard stills and bathtubs, and an astonishing array of business establishments. A New York newspaper listed thirty-odd points of purchase, including dancing schools, paint stores, restaurants, and moving companies. In anticipation of a parched drinking future, the wealthy stored up on a lot of the good stuff. "I find that people expect more [liquor] at a dinner party than before Prohibition," a woman wrote to her ex-husband, Secretary of the Treasury Andrew Mellon. She wanted advice on how to move bootleg scotch from her summer home to her winter one.

The French 75 remained part of the cocktail equation. If readers think back to Judge Jr. (illustrator Norman Hume Anthony), they will recall his *Here's How!*, which foreshadowed Harry Craddock's French 75. It appeared in 1927, the height of Prohibition. Another one of his cocktail books during this time was ironically titled *Noble Experiments*.

That cocktailing carried through Repeal in 1933 should not have been a surprise. Drinking illegally was exciting. No finger can plug a dike meant to hold back booze. This has not only been the case with American dikes. France banned absinthe in 1915. Nevertheless, the green fairy was an ingredient in McElhone's *ABC of Cocktails* French 75. Enforcement was chiefly on production, not on serving, says Brian Robinson, the proprietor of the Wormwood Society. A bartender could draw from unused stock or import absinthe from countries where it was not banned.

What happened after Repeal, however, was unexpected. Cocktail culture did not come roaring back. Per capita alcohol consumption remained below pre-Prohibition levels and stayed that way for years. Also, tastes changed.

The French 75 was still served. The *Stork Club Bar Book,* which appeared in 1946, featured it. The book said the cocktail was "enshrined in the pharmacopoeia of alcohol artistry." But New York City's Stork Club was not an accurate barometer of American drinking tastes. This was a place, after all, where Ernest Hemingway cashed a $100,000 royalty check to pay for his drinks one night.

While John Wayne may have kept the name of the French 75 alive in movie theaters, people in the post–World War II John Wayne culture drank the way he supposedly did in real life: copious amounts of Wild Turkey. The Mai Tai cocktail briefly caught fire. The most significant development was an interest in vodka cocktails, hardly a daring drink choice.

Then, at the turn of the century, cocktails entered a new golden age. Harry McElhone's *ABC of Mixing Cocktails* and *The Savoy Cocktail Book* were pulled off the shelf. Restaurants began to think of cocktails as an extension of their food menus, which were becoming more imaginative.

Liquor company advertisements encouraged people to order cocktails or mix them at home. In 2000, the United States had a total of twenty-four distilleries; twenty years later more than two thousand distilleries made spirits. Bars dedicated to the careful execution of handmade cocktails sprang up.

The pulse of this renaissance was particularly strong in New Orleans, where the French 75 previously had been an afterthought.

A SHOT-GLASS-SIZE HISTORY OF DRINKING IN THE CRESCENT CITY

In New York you have Macy's Thanksgiving Parade. It lasts a few hours. In New Orleans you have Mardi Gras parades. They go on for days. How many bar books have the names of a city in their titles? If New Orleans isn't tops, it's close to the top. It punches above its weight in bar books and drinking.

It matters less that New Orleans did not invent the word *cocktail* than that so many New Orleanians persist in saying that it did, in a shop at 437 Royal Street. In the 1830s this French Quarter pharmacy belonged to Antoine Amédée Peychaud, whose bitters spiced up brandy. According to legend, he served the drink in a cup called a *coquetier*. One of the city's more likely contributions to cocktail culture was the free lunch. This brainstorm originated in the Café des Réfugiés as a way to bring in more drinking customers. This idea was copied nationally. The list goes on. We can't say for sure who invented the "go cup," but the French Quarter perfected its use.

New Orleans was resilient in the face of Prohibition. Izzy Einstein, an eminent federal agent on the hooch watch, deemed New Orleans the city in which alcoholic drinks were the easiest to find. Local police, who were supposed to help Einstein, were known for siding with the drinkers, besides making moonshine themselves.

Celebrated cocktails hail from New Orleans. In his brilliant *The Gentleman's Companion: Being an Exotic Drinking Book; or, Around the World with Jigger, Beaker and Flask* (1939), Charles Baker spoke of the "immortal Sazarac." He found quite a number of New Orleans fizzes to his taste, especially the Ramos Gin Fizz, created in 1888 and "synonymous with the finest in all the New Orleans art." Around the same time, Stanley Clisby Arthur wrote *Famous New Orleans Drinks & How to Make 'Em*. The book called out the Absinthe Frappé (originating at the Old Absinthe House), the Place d'Armes cocktail, the Roffignac (Roffignac being the tenth mayor of the city) cocktail, the Vieux Carré cocktail, and the Tchoupitoulas Street Guzzle (a street name difficult to pronounce even when sober).

These excursions into New Orleans cocktails do not have a word about the French 75. Old bar menus in the New Orleans Historic Collection say only slightly more. The French 75 was not routinely on the cocktail list at Galatoire's, Brennan's, Napoleon House, Commander's Palace, and other iconic New Orleans restaurants.

A 1939 *New Orleans Times-Picayune* feature story recounted the story of three men who decided to soothe themselves with French 75s after a sad day at the racetrack. After partaking at a hotel bar, one of them recounted,

"Tony fell three times in the lobby and Andy got mixed up in some palm trees. But I didn't think anything of it. I was busy trying to get out of the swing door at the front of the joint." The drink was an offbeat adventure for the three gents and apparently for the bartender as well. According to the press account, he made the French 75 with rum "and a few other things."

"We were always pushing the New Orleans eye-openers," says Ti Martin, co-owner of Commander's Palace, referring to the Bloody Marys and milk punches people downed at Sunday morning brunch after a long night. The French 75 was not one of the city's quintessential drinks.

Until, Arnaud's French 75 Bar became, in David Wondrich's words, "one of the stations of the cross of the modern cocktail cult."

ARNAUD'S

I met Katy Casbarian at Arnaud's on a fall afternoon, a few hours before customers filled the restaurant. She was wear-

ing a dark cotton dress with faux double-breasted front—like the restaurant, comfortable and dignified. The first thing one recognizes about her, after her easy laugh, is her respect for the history of the French Quarter restaurant her family acquired in 1979.

Arnaud's is a history book. Each of the seventeen dining rooms is a chapter. Altogether eleven buildings on Bienville Street were cobbled onto the original. There's the Count's Room, named after "Count" Arnaud Cazenave, who opened the restaurant in 1918; the Jazz Bistro, formerly the Richelieu Room; and the Main Dining Room, which makes Katy Casbarian laugh. "It is so basic compared to the names of every other space that we have." We talked in the one-table alcove named the Bacchus Room.

Upstairs is the Germaine Cazenave Wells Mardi Gras Museum. Wells was Arnaud's daughter and became owner after he died in 1948. She was said to have been queen in more than twenty Mardi Gras balls from 1937 to 1968. The museum has Mardi Gras costumes, including hers and

Opposite: The Arnaud's French 75. [Photo by Sam Gregory Anselmo]

her father's when he was a Mardi Gras king. She was a would-be opera singer known for grand entrances.

Arnaud Cazenave came to New Orleans from France. He was a wine merchant with a knack for public relations, his "count" title being a good example. His restaurant became a French Quarter culinary landmark, with plenty of good stories.

During Prohibition the service bar in the kitchen carried on. Customers entered from an alley and drank amid the pots and pans. In the dining room, others sipped from coffee cups. The count was arrested once, Katy Casbarian reminisces. She isn't sure if he went to jail briefly or got off entirely. The city's judges were good customers.

By the end of Germaine Wells's stewardship, Arnaud's had declined into roof-leaking decrepitation. Archie Casbarian and his wife Jane leased the restaurant and then bought it. Ms. Wells lived upstairs until she died in 1983.

It may seem curious that an Egyptian-born Armenian hotelier trained in Switzerland bought a landmark Creole restaurant. But as *New Yorker* reporter A. J. Liebling wrote, "New Orleans resembles Genoa or Marseilles, or Beirut or the Egyptian Alexandria more than it does New York." And that does not include the Spanish roots of the city, the Irish policemen who patrolled the streets when Liebling was there in the 1950s, and the Scandinavian sailors who disembarked ships in the port by the thousands each year.

The Casbarians were determined to revive the restaurant in a way that respected its past, even if they had to make changes to do so. One of those changes was to the Men's Grill, which, as the name implies, was a male preserve. They changed it in 1979 into the women-welcome Grill Bar and renovated it with antiques that harkened back to the restaurant's beginnings. The masterpiece is the 1800s vintage back bar. The Casbarians wanted to make a cocktail refuge off busy Bienville and Bourbon Streets. It was supposed to "feel like you were in Paris," Katy Casbarian says.

The Casbarians made another change in 2003. They renamed the Grill Bar the French 75 Bar. This was one more instance of adopting the French 75 name because of how it sounds to the ear, not because of the cocktail's World War I fame or its taste. Jane Casbarian suggested the name because, her daughter says, it "fit in with the decor of the rest of the restaurant, which had a French flair." As part of the overhaul the Casbarians came up with their own version of the French 75.

In what seems to be an effort to make history conform to the present, it is sometimes said that the French 75 was a favorite of Count Arnaud. Katy Casbarian thinks that is malarkey. It is true that Germaine Wells is known to have sipped the gin-Champagne variety. But the cocktail held no special place in the restaurant. When it was on the menu, it was not printed in red ink, as was reserved for "Our Own Creations," for instance Arnaud's "Special Cocktail," consisting of Scotch, Dubonnet, and orange bitters. When William Grimes of the *New York Times* "charted the globe on a cocktail napkin" in 1998, he included Arnaud's as one of those bars that spoke "with a local accent." A photo with the story showed head bartender Bobby Oakes shaking a Ramos Gin Fizz.

The Casbarians did a lot of testing (e.g., drinking) to come up with a French 75 they liked. They eventually decided on Cognac, which Archie Casbarian sipped constantly in the evenings. They kept the sugar, lemon, and Champagne that were in Germaine Wells's French 75.

This was not a brand-new drink. An earlier version, for instance, can be found in David Embury's *The Fine Art of Mixing Drinks,* published half a century before. But the new bar and the new drink created a buzz when they premiered together. The decibel level increased further after the Casbarians hired Chris Hannah in 2004. Hannah, a shy, compact man with a close-shaved pate and intense dark eyes, was into the new cocktail culture and good at what he did. He imposed precision on the mixing of Arnaud's French 75 and became a missionary for the cocktail. The ambitious bartender, says Bobby Oakes, who mentored Hannah, put the bar on the "must visit list."

"The French 75 cocktail had a journey to becoming the New Orleans cocktail," Hannah told me. "I feel like I wrote the story. It's what I am known for." He dug into old New Orleans cocktail books, none of which, he said, had a French 75 recipe. To make the case that Cognac is the orig-

Chris Hannah mixes a French 75 at Arnaud's. [Photo by Denny Culvert]

inal ingredient, he innocently draws on Jean Shepherd's half-baked story about its invention by aviation ace Raoul Lufbery of the Lafayette Escadrille.

Arnaud's French 75 was not met with universal approbation by the cocktail intelligentsia. The dispute was reminiscent of the Western Schism of the fourteenth and fifteenth centuries. This was when two Catholic prelates claimed to be the duly elected pope. Ted Haigh, known as Dr. Cocktail, is a staunch member of the Savoy School. Of Hannah's French 75, he wrote categorically in *Vintage Spirits and Forgotten Cocktails,* "If this drink has any problem, it is the misapprehension that it correctly contains brandy (Cognac) instead of gin. It is an error that has been frequently repeated in various bar guides over time." Dr. Cocktail says the Cognac version is "properly designated the French 125." Arnaud's calls its gin version the French 95.

It took forty years for the two-pope crisis to be resolved. The 75 Schism may never end, although it should. As with the Western Schism, which resulted in a third party sitting in St. Peter's Chair, neither side has it quite right.

Apple-based distillate was used in the first recorded recipes, as we have seen. This was not Cognac, but it was brandy. Arnaud's cocktail's connection with the first 75s is close enough to give Hannah three-quarters of a point on this part of the drink's history.

There is more, however, to be considered. None of the critics, so far as I can discern, touched on the real weakness of Hannah's claim. The early drinks did not have Champagne, as Arnaud's and Dr. Cocktail's do. Also neither of these latter drinks has grenadine, and Arnaud's does not have gin, both of which the earliest ones did. That's a zero for both sides insofar as historical purity is concerned.

Hannah's crusade and the conflict that resulted was good for the French 75, not bad. It brought more attention to the cocktail. Everyone likes a good fight. Cocktail writer Wayne Curtis remembers an enjoyable night in January 2005 watching Hannah and Haigh engage in genteel trash-talking over Arnaud's bar.

But does the argument matter? At this point in L'Affaire des Soixante-Quinze, we know debates like this miss the point. Arnaud's created a superb French 75 with notes of the past. "The most refined version of a French 75 is with Cognac," Katy Casbarian told me. "It looks the best. It tastes the best. It is the best. And that is what I have to say about that." While this is a matter of taste, not history, the fact is that the cocktail "blows the others right out of the water" at Arnaud's. It sells ten-to-one against other mixed drinks. For her family's restaurant, Casbarian says, "It will forever be the shining star."

Archie Casbarian died in 2009. Katy and her brother Archie took over Arnaud's. Hannah continued to build the reputation of the French 75 Bar as well as enhance his own. The partnership led to Arnaud's winning the 2017 James Beard Award for Outstanding Bar Program, a culinary honor equated with the Oscars for movies. Hannah, who went out on his own the next year, became a partner in the Jewel of the South, a restaurant and bar a few streets away from Arnaud's. The French 75 is one of its signature drinks. In 1922 Hannah won the Tales of the Cocktail Spirited Award for U.S. Bartender of the Year.

"I strongly believe," Katy Casbarian says of Arnaud's partnership with Hannah, "that the synergy accounts in large part for the repopularization of the French 75."

THE REPOPULARIZATION OF
THE FRENCH 75

Today no serious New Orleans cocktail book ignores the French 75. The authors of *Cure: New Orleans Drinks and How to Mix 'Em* call the drink "a core part of the New Orleans cocktail canon." *Lift Your Spirits: A Celebratory History of Cocktail Culture in New Orleans* treats the French 75 as though it always belonged there. The cocktail, the authors write, has "a feel of old New Orleans." In the city's famed restaurant bars it is often one of the top three drinks.

The surge of the French 75 in New Orleans, moreover, has contributed to its resurgence outside the city limits. We can trace the ripple effects that spread out from Arnaud's French 75 Bar.

First, Arnaud's introduced the drink. "This," Bobby Oakes says, "realigned people's opinions." Other New Orleans bars fell into step. When the line at Arnaud's bar door grew too long, someone thirsty for a French 75 could get one down the street, which some bars satisfied by offering both Arnaud's Cognac style and the Savoy gin style.

The popularity of the cocktail in New Orleans would by itself have elevated the drink nationally. New Orleans is a prime destination for visitors with a keen appetite for food and drink. They return home evangelists. Think how Paul Prudhomme's blackened redfish started a national trend.

But an event in 2002 was a booster rocket for the French 75. This was the launching of Tales of the Cocktail, which has grown into an annual event attracting thousands of bartenders eager to swap stories and watch expert bartenders mix their specialties. Chris Hannah was a "landmark" in the event, says cocktail writer Wayne Curtis, who came to the city to do a story and stayed. This education process became more formal several years later with the creation of a Cocktail Apprentice Program. Curtis credits

Tales of the Cocktail with showcasing the French 75 to the wider world.

New Orleans bartenders are remarkably cooperative. The city is a good place for budding bartenders to learn their trade. It does not hurt, either, that the Museum of the American Cocktail opened in New Orleans in 2008. It hosts traveling exhibits and gives annual awards—called olives—to bars and bartenders.

In due course one could find the French 75 on a bar menu in Atlanta or San Francisco with a credit line noting it hailed from Arnaud's or was made Chris Hannah's way. Other familiar iterations of the cocktail have been lifted up as well, to the point that the French 75 is now a standard, rather than a curiosity, across the country. Here is how it is treated by Meaghan Dorman, owner of Raines Law Room and other New York City bars and an outstanding cocktail creator known for her magic with Champagne. When she tests a new gin, she tries it in a Martini and a French 75. "It better be good," she told me over lunch one day, or she won't clutter the bar shelves with it.

Dorman believes the country is undergoing a second modern upsurge of interest in cocktails. The touchstone is classic cocktails, she said; the French 75 has never before been the object of so much collective creativity. A welter of variations has appeared, some good and some not.

Start with New Orleans. Cure, an award-winning bar opened in 2009 by *Cure* cocktail book co-author Neal Bodenheimer, serves its French 75 with a different brandy than Arnaud's and uses *crémant* instead of Champagne. Luke, another local restaurant, pours a French 75 in a brandy glass with egg whites and triple sec. Antoine's offers a number of versions, including a newly invented Empress Tiger. The cocktail refers to Louisiana State University's mascot and depicts the school's colors. The purple Empress gin and golden Champagne do not mix, literally or figuratively. It looks like an ice cream parfait and only has value as an Instagram photo. I've had a French 75 at the Old Absinthe House, whose booze slinger that day had no idea the drink worked with absinthe and served a Champagne and gin concoction with as much personality as a glass of water.

Outside New Orleans, the pattern repeats itself. Of the three French 75 versions served in the French 75 Lounge and Art Gallery in Aurora, one is Braden Smith's creation: brandy, lemon juice, grenadine, and sparkling rosé. *The Essential New York Times Book of Cocktails* calls attention to a French 75 riff called a German 71; the name comes from a German World Cup victory over Brazil, score 7–1. It uses sparkling Riesling instead of Champagne. Someone else pushes a Blood Orange French 75. The self-styled holy book of imbibing, *Cocktail: The Drinks Bible for the 21st Century,* says the French 75 uses Cointreau instead of sugar. One of the more attractive 75 inventions comes from the Atlas bar in Singapore. Among other twists, it uses a Sri Lanka gin made with curry leaves. The recipe is found at the end of chapter 6.

I confess, my son and I convinced a bartender in Trondheim, Norway, to try a French 75 with aquavit. It was awful. I later saw an aquavit recipe on a website, but that does not give much reassurance. As the revival of cocktails has progressed, Wayne Curtis ruefully told me, "It has become a parody of itself." Think of French 75 jello shots (as much as I prefer not to) or the French 75 Pitcher with demi-sec Champagne and maraschino cherries, or French 75s with rhubarb or blackberry liqueur, or some sort of jam, or frozen French 75s, or the oxymoronic spiked cannon version of the French 75, which is nonalcoholic.

L'Affaire des Soixante-Quinze, however, cannot end on dispiriting notes. We need a nightcap that celebrates the French 75's elasticity, its essential quality. For more than a century, the 75 mm field piece has mobilized delicious, if dizzying experimentation. We'll call the nightcap chapter, which contains some of the best recipes, the "canon of the cannon."

CHAPTER SIX

THE CANON
OF THE CANNON

The versatile French 75 makes itself at home in well-worn Harry's New York Bar and at the chic Savoy. The cocktail lived it up one afternoon in Commander's Palace in New Orleans's Garden District.

I first met Dan Davis, Commander's spirited head of spirits, during a Saturday lunch. A jazz band swayed through the balloon-filled second-floor dining room, which looked on the garden patio. Waiters and their supervisors patrolled the room searching for the enemy: improperly aligned silverware or a frown on a customer's face.

Davis oversees the restaurant's wine and cocktail program with verve. At the University of New Orleans, he likes to say, "I studied history but majored in the French Quarter." When I told him about my investigation of L'Affaire des Soixante-Quinze, he said, "Let's taste 'em."

Our historical tour of the cocktail took place a few days later in Commander's wine room, which is lined with wine bottles and has a dining table made out of lacquered caramel-colored wine cases. Davis's bar accoutrements, spread on the table, were as sparkling and tidy as a display case at Tiffany's. With us was Ti Adelaide Martin, Commander's co-owner and coauthor—both with her cousin Lally Brennan—of *In the Land of Cocktails*. This cocktail book has the Arnaud's and the Savoy versions for the French 75, both of which Commander's also serves. Ti Martin says family members drank French 75s before the cocktail enjoyed its recent renaissance.

We started with the original Soixante-Quinze mentioned in 1915. Applejack, Davis explained, had advanced from a cider-based spirit that was "jacked" by freezing in order to isolate the alcohol content. It was distilled and closer to what we think of as Calvados. Davis had acquired Holman Applejack, the only American applejack distilled by traditional methods. The applejack version of the drink, which Davis mixed, was cloyingly sweet. "Many palates at the time would have equated sweetness with quality," he said. The drink did well to progress quickly into other forms.

The same can be said for the Difford's recipe with Old Tom, a sweet gin that was hugely popular long ago. It is one of those drinks, Davis observed, "that yells out, 'I dare you to like it because it is cool.'" We didn't take the dare.

What follows is based on the afternoon with Davis and my own French 75 experiences. I express my preferences on the drinks explicitly and indirectly. Regarding the latter, for instance, I ignore the elderflower form of the cocktail, whose sweetness eliminates it from the list.

These recipes attempt to be faithful to the original, but I have had to make adjustments and suppositions. Sometimes, for instance, original measurements are not clearly defined. I have shown measurements first in milliliters out of respect for the international character of the cocktail and second in approximate U.S. ounces (in parentheses).

HARRY'S ORIGINAL 75

This is the cocktail that appeared for the first time in Harry McElhone's *ABC of Mixing Cocktails*. [It is misremembered in a recent edition of the book produced by his descendants.] For measurements, McElhone called for 2/3 Calvados and 1/3 gin. His instructions include a drawing of a double-sided jigger, with one end labeled "two-thirds" and the other "one-third." Together they probably held two ounces. Around this time a cocktail was normally this amount, notes David Wondrich. Cocktails are generally larger today, and I have stated the recipe accordingly.

One teaspoonful grenadine [5 ml]

Two dashes of absinthe

60 ml [2 oz] Calvados

30 ml [1 oz] gin

Shake well with ice and strain into a cocktail glass. A coupe is better. No garnish.

Robert Vermeire did not use absinthe and reversed the gin and Calvados proportions. This was one of Davis's favorites. Davis also made a version from Difford's online guide that used star anise as a garnish. Ti Martin thought the French 75 should not have absinthe. "It's not what it is supposed to taste like," she said. I differ, but the anise garnish is too strong.

Laurent Giraud, the maître de bar at Harry's Bar, says this about the absinthe: "You're supposed to wash the glass with some absinthe—a little dash. Then you throw the rest away. We just add a little of the freshness that we need. Absinthe is very powerful. Let's make sure that it doesn't take over everything."

HARRY'S NEW 75

The drink served today at Harry's—let's call it Harry's New 75—substitutes Champagne for Calvados but retains its distinctive absinthe wash. The recipe came verbally from Laurent Giraud.

40 ml (1 1/3 oz) London dry gin
20 ml (2/3 oz) fresh lemon juice
15 ml (1/2 oz) simple syrup
Dash of absinthe

Shake well with ice and strain into a coupe. Top with brut Champagne. No garnish.

I like a strong London dry gin with both of Harry's 75s. Harry's New York Bar uses 90 proof Fords. Navy-strength Plymouth gin weighs in at 114 proof. After all, the drink is named after a cannon, not a popgun.

THE SAVOY'S 75

"Now we get to the Champagne!" Dan Davis declared. He started with Judge Jr.'s recipe, which was elevated in fame by Harry Craddock and *The Savoy Cocktail Book*. It is a good summer drink, where the original Harry's is more like a Manhattan.

40 ml (1 1/3 oz) gin
20 ml (2/3 oz) lemon juice
One teaspoon of powdered sugar

Shake well. Pour into a tall glass with cracked ice and fill with brut Champagne. No garnish. (My advice is to deviate from the Savoy recipe; shake the gin, lemon juice, and sugar with ice, pour into Champagne flute, and add the Champagne.)

"I love the drink," Davis said. "I love highly acidic drinks." For the fun of it, he also made up a similar cocktail, dubbing it the Commander's French 75. The chief difference was the addition of Cognac. It was a good lesson: You can be creative and build a drink to your taste.

ARNAUD'S 75

This is the recipe created by the Casbarians and promoted by Chris Hannah. Occasionally the recipes on Arnaud's website change slightly. This one is from a May 2011 video of Hannah making the drink.

30 ml (1 oz) Cognac
7.5 ml (1/4 oz) lemon juice
7.5 ml (1/4 oz) simple syrup
Top with about 60 ml (2 oz) brut Champagne

Place the Cognac, lemon juice, and simple syrup in a shaker filled with ice. Shake to chill and pour into a tulip Champagne glass; add the Champagne, garnish with a lemon twist.

Contrary to the view that it is pointless to use high-quality ingredients in a mixed drink, better ingredients do make better drinks. Davis remade Arnaud's version with a rare Cognac. It moved the taste up a couple of notches. Of course, the price would have gone up many notches. Dauphine's in Washington DC offers such a French 75 for two. It costs $150. Courvoisier VS, which Arnaud's uses, is a reasonably priced good Cognac.

Price is not as much a consideration when it comes to other ingredients. With grenadine, it is essential to stay away from cheap brands made with cornstarch, food coloring, and flavoring. The increase in cost is minimal and the benefit to the drink is monumental. Lemon juice always should be freshly squeezed.

THE FRENCH 75
À LA FOUNTAIN INN

This bar is around the corner from my home in Georgetown, Washington, DC. The cocktail, invented on the premises, combines old and new versions of Harry's French 75s. The inclusion of many ingredients is often a recipe for disaster, but this works.

15 ml (1/2 oz) Calvados
15 ml (1/2 oz) gin
30 ml (1 oz) lemon juice
15 ml (1/2 oz) simple syrup
7.5 ml (1/4 oz) grenadine
1.25 ml (1/4 tsp) absinthe

Shake with ice, pour into flute, and top with about 45 ml (1.5 oz) brut Champagne.

THE ATLAS FRENCH 75

This drink comes from a bar by that name in Singapore. It is proud of its 1,400 varieties of gin and its collection of Champagne. Their French 75 recipe shows once again how much creative juice and promotional pizzazz can be brought to the drink.

1 dash saline solution (they use a 1:10 salt to water solution)
20 ml (2/3 oz) fresh lemon juice
15 ml (1/2 oz) simple syrup
10 ml (1/3 oz) crème de pêche
40 ml (1 1/3 oz) London dry gin
20 ml (2/3 oz) floral Champagne

The bar uses Colombo No. 7 gin, which has seven spices including curry leaf. But any London dry will work, says Lidiyanah "Yana" K, the head bartender.

The final stage of mixing the drink is done tableside. Yana, who began her career in advertising, calls this an Instagram moment. The show, such as it is, involves the bartender pouring the Champagne into a flute with a candied kumquat and adding the other, previously shaken ingredients. It is not as dazzling as Jerry Thomas's flaming blue blazer, passed back and forth from silver shakers, but the drink is sunny. It is also about as far away from the original French 75 of 1915 as one can get.

CONCLUSION

L'Affaire des Quatorze in eighteenth-century France began with a poem. In their search for the culprit, the French police found culprits and a proliferation of subversive verse. With L'Affaire des Soixante-Quinze, it is the same. There is no French 75. There are French 75s. This book ends with a poetic toast to the elusive drink.

A TOAST TO THE FRENCH 75

To the Soixante-Quinze,
And its elusive past.
Like the French cannons,
This cocktail fires fast.

Unknown the prime progenitor,
No rules on what it must contain.
You may make it non-sequitur,
It never needs to be the same.

Gin today; tomorrow Champagne.
Nix the brandy, liqueur makes merry.
You may launch a *coup de main,*
By pouring in a little green fairy.

It's according to your taste,
And if you want minds blown,
It's an honor, not a disgrace,
To flout Craddock or McElhone.

To the Soixante-Quinze!
The drink for an iconoclast.
Named for French cannons,
This cocktail is a blast.

ACKNOWLEDGMENTS

In 2023, an Italo-American archaeological team announced their discovery of a five-thousand-year-old tavern in Lagash, an ancient city in southern Iraq. A cuneiform tablet found among the ruins carried a recipe for beer, which the team believed to be the bar's most popular beverage, even exceeding water. Photos showed piles of broken pottery "mugs" strewn about. The Lagash Lounge must have held a hell of a party the night it closed down.

Based on research for this book, I feel confident that the Lagash Lounge's mixologist claimed this was the place where beer was invented. As soon as there were bars, there was fake news.

Writing this book, I came to embrace the frustrations of sorting facts from fakes. The fakes are an integral part of the story. At the same time, it was a happy relief to find reliable sources in print and in person.

The names of useful books and articles appear in the foregoing pages. One that is not mentioned and deserves praise is *The Oxford Companion to Spirits and Cocktails* (editor-in-chief David Wondrich). I also used other Wondrich books, such as *Imbibe,* and I much appreciated the advice and clarifications he gave via email.

Robert Darnton's fine book on L'Affaire des Quatorze is *Poetry and the Police.* Background on the Mamie Taylor Cocktail came from Eric Felten's article in the *Wall Street Journal* (July 19, 2008). Buckmaster's recollections on his club are in "The Story of Buck's," *Town and Country,* February 1947. Two scholarly articles guided me on the French 75 cannon: Robert Kaplan, "Making Sense of the Rennes Verdict: The Military Dimension of the Dreyfus Affair," *Journal of Contemporary History* (1999), and David Stevenson, "The Field Artillery Revolution and the European Military Balance, 1890–1914," *International History Review* (2018). Of exceptional value on the propaganda inspired by the cannon is "La Fabuleuse Historie du Canon de 75 Modèle

1897." It can be found at https://canonde75modele1897
.blogspot.com. As a result of research for a previous book,
*Manipulating the Masses: Woodrow Wilson and the Birth of
American Propaganda,* I knew about and used E. Alexander
Powell's papers in the Manuscript Division of the Library
of Congress.

Journalist and New Orleans bon vivant John Pope introduced me to Dan Davis at Commander's Palace. Kit
Wohl, who has written on New Orleans food and drink,
connected me to Katy Casbarian. Thanks to them all. I
thank Major Rupert Lendrum for letting me into Buck's
Club, and ebullient Susan Scott, the Savoy archivist, for
giving me so much time.

Cocktail writer Wayne Curtis and cocktail creator Meaghan Dorman commented on the manuscript in draft, as
did longtime friends, who have been acknowledged in
previous books: Bob Mong, Rob Regh, and Jack Sullivan.
Sullivan's popular blog "pre-prowhiskeymen@blogspot
.com" carried an article about my great-grandfather, "Tom
Curran and The Three Orphans Saloon" (February 21,
2021). Brian Robinson of the Wormwood Society taught

me about absinthe and secured navy strength No. 7 Colombo gin so we could try the Atlas French 75 as it was meant to be served. Other help came from Polly Russell, who leads the Eccles Centre for American Studies at the British Library and coauthored an article with me on the French 75 for the *Independent;* my graduate assistant Olivia Romaguera and two of her fellow graduate students, Katie Bailey and Caroline Cantrelle; and my curiosity-driven friend Elena Pehrkon, who unearthed important details that I would have missed. Viyas Sundaram generously arranged a public tasting of French 75s at the Fountain Inn. Alisa Plant and the entire LSU Press staff were superb, as usual.

Finally, I thank my son, Maxwell, for drinking with me; my daughter-in-law, Silvia Spring, for editing advice; and Bettsie Miller, for polishing the manuscript (although annoyingly cutting the word *neologistics*) and for inspiration of all kinds.

ICONIC NEW ORLEANS COCKTAILS

The Sazerac
The Café Brûlot
The Vieux Carré
The Absinthe Frappé
The French 75